MAORI

Robert Macdonald

Wayland

Titles in the series

Australian Aborigines
Bedouin
Inuit
Kurds
Maori
Native Americans
Rainforest Amerindians
Saami of Lapland
San of the Kalahari
Tibetans

Minority Rights Group

This book has been produced in consultation with the Minority Rights Group; an international non-governmental organization working to secure justice for ethnic, linguistic, religious and social minorities worldwide who are suffering discrimination.

The title page shows the legendary departure of the ancestors of the Maori. They navigated their twin-hulled canoes from a homeland called *Hawaiki*.

Series editor: Paul Mason
Designer: Kudos Editorial and Design Services

Picture acknowledgements
The artwork on pages 5 and 40 was supplied by Peter Bull. The publishers gratefully acknowledge the permission of the following to use their pictures: Mary Evans Picture Library 6, 8, 20, 21, 32, 33 bottom; Eye Ubiquitous 4, 7, 10, 11, 12, 15, 16, 17, 18, 19, 23, 24, 25, 26, 27, 28, 31, 33 top, 34, 37, 38, 39, 41, 43, 44 both; Hutchison 35; Lifefile 22, 30, 45; Robert MacDonald 13, 36; Topham 42; Wayland 14, 29.

First published in 1993 by
Wayland (Publishers) Ltd
61 Western Rd, Hove
East Sussex BN3 1JD, England

British Library Cataloguing in Publication Data
MacDonald, Robert
   Maori.- (Threatened Cultures Series)
   I. Title II. Series
   305.89

ISBN 0-7502-0503-2

Typeset by Malcolm Walker of Kudos Design
Printed and bound by Lego, Italy

Contents

Aotearoa - New Zealand

Nobody knows for sure how the Maori got to New Zealand hundreds of years ago. They live on two very big islands in the South Pacific, on the edge of the great Southern Ocean – islands all by themselves in an enormous sea. There are no other countries close to New Zealand, or *Aotearoa*, as the Maori called the country: Australia is the nearest neighbour. Almost two thousand kilometres of water separate the two – the Tasman Sea, which is one of the stormiest.

Scholars once believed that a great fleet of Polynesian sailing canoes brought the ancestors of most of the modern Maori to *Aotearoa* from a distant Pacific island homeland, called *Hawaiki*. People have studied Maori legends more closely recently. It seems likely that some of the ancestral canoes named in the legends came not from the distant Pacific but from another part of *Aotearoa* itself.

▼ *Maori in New Zealand's Northland province still put to sea in this great war canoe on ceremonial occasions. The canoes which first brought their ancestors to Aotearoa may have been double this size – two hulls joined together with a sailing platform between them.*

According to Maori legend, the North Island of *Aotearoa* was fished up from the sea bed by a hero called Maui-Tikitiki-a-Taranga. They call the North Island Te-Ika-a-Maui (The Fish of Maui). If you look at a map you will see that it does look like a fish of the ray family. The Mahia Peninsula juts out from the east coast and the Maori say it is Maui's fish-hook, which he made from his grandmother's jawbone. Maui's brothers tried to chop the fish up. That is why the country is covered in long mountain ranges.

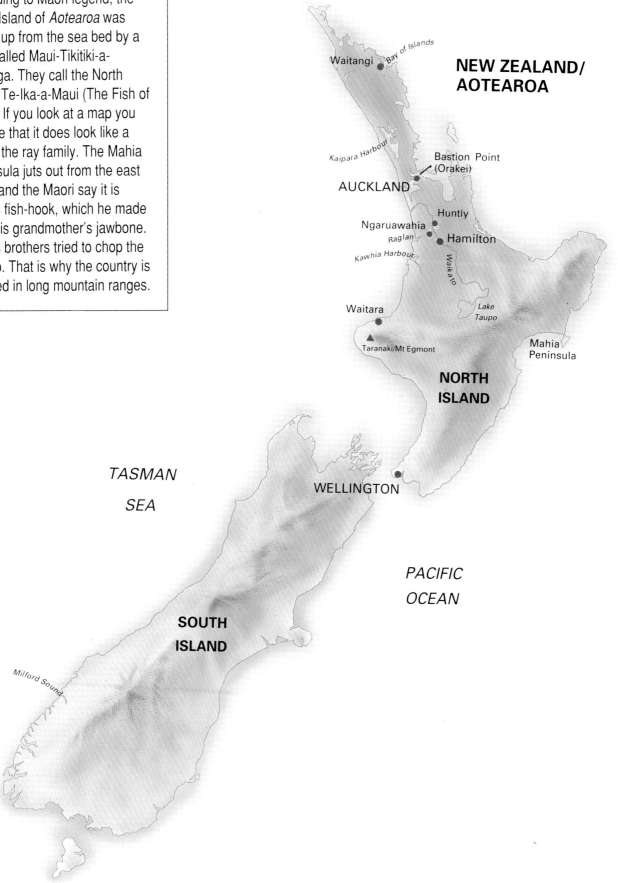

NEW ZEALAND/ AOTEAROA

Waitangi   Bay of Islands

Kaipara Harbour

Bastion Point (Orakei)

AUCKLAND

Huntly

Ngaruawahia
Raglan   Hamilton
Kawhia Harbour

Waikato

Waitara

Lake Taupo

Mahia Peninsula

Taranaki/Mt Egmont

NORTH ISLAND

TASMAN

SEA

WELLINGTON

PACIFIC

OCEAN

SOUTH ISLAND

Milford Sound

To the north are the warm waters of the Pacific and the islands of Polynesia, where people live who are closely related in their language and culture to the New Zealand Maoris. But the nearest of these island groups is almost as far away as Australia. The only large neighbour to the south is Antarctica: a continent of ice and snow inhabited by penguins and seals.

Two thousand years ago there were no people living in New Zealand, and no animals. It was a land of birds. Somewhere around AD 750 the first human beings arrived. They came from the islands of Eastern Polynesia. The Polynesians were adventurous explorers of the Pacific, who travelled from island to island on great sea-going canoes, with hulls made from two tree-trunks joined together and with matting sails.

Were the Polynesians looking for a new country in the Southern Ocean, or did they discover New Zealand by accident after being blown off course? We will never know.

When people first arrived in *Aotearoa* they found about a dozen different kinds of heavy flightless bird: the largest of these might stand four metres tall. The Maori called these birds the *moa*. They were hunted almost to extinction by the earliest people in *Aotearoa*, who were called the *Moa* Hunters by Victorian archaeologists. Because they were similar people to the Maori, the *Moa* Hunters are now known as the Archaic Maori. There may have been a few small *moa* still alive when the first European explorers arrived, but no Pakeha (non-Maori) has ever seen a *moa*.

▲   *Giant trees, nikau palms and tall tree-ferns grew in Aotearoa's dense forests, which covered much of the country until settlers arrived from Europe in the nineteenth century. The Europeans cut and burned the forests to make farmland.*

OLD AOTEAROA

Maori tribal legends are full of stories of great voyages and of a distant homeland called *Hawaiki*. They called New Zealand *Aotearoa*, which means the Land of the Long White Cloud. This is how the first voyagers saw New Zealand on the horizon - a long shining cloud covering the hills and mountains.

The first arrivals lived by fishing and by hunting the giant flightless birds, known as *moa*, which were common in New Zealand then. As the population increased tribes began to grow plants brought from the Pacific, but these were hard to cultivate in *Aotearoa*'s colder climate.

Because the country was so isolated the Maori developed over the centuries a way of life which was very different from the one their ancestors had left behind in the distant Polynesian islands to the north. *Aotearoa*'s forests contained some of the largest trees in the world, and the Maori became great wood-carvers. The men became great fighters too, for tribal warfare was a habit among the Maori. It was treated almost like a favourite sport and every warrior sought to gain prestige in battle.

The first Pakeha

When Pakeha first came to the Kaipara Harbour in the north of New Zealand the Ngati Whatua chief Paikea Te Hekeua told them: *'We are all the children of the great Queen Victoria. You are my Pakehas, and I and my tribe will be ever ready to protect you with our bodies. You have much to teach us, and you may learn things from us that will be useful to you. May we be brothers for ever.'*

▲   *The signing of the Treaty of Waitangi in 1840 marked the end of old Aotearoa and the start of modern New Zealand, as the Maori agreed to place themselves under the protection of the British queen.*

ARRIVAL OF THE PAKEHA

Of course nowadays the Maori no longer fight in this way among themselves. Their way of life has changed almost completely in the last 150 years. The main cause of this change was the arrival of white explorers and then white settlers in *Aotearoa*. They called the country New Zealand and they saw that it had magnificent forests full of valuable timber, land which would be easy to farm and seas teeming with fish and other life. In the early nineteenth century more and more people from Europe and America travelled to New Zealand, and many tried to buy land from the Maori. The Maori called these white people Pakeha, or strangers, and at first they were keen to learn from them about Western inventions.

The Maori wanted to know about the Pakeha's farming methods and other skills, and they welcomed Pakeha traders. The Pakeha population got bigger, and in 1840 the British queen, Victoria, suggested to the Maori that *Aotearoa* should become a British colony. Maori chiefs were told that if they signed a treaty with the queen they would always be able to keep their lands, forests and fisheries. No one would take the Maori's lands away from them. Neither the British government nor the Maori knew how many settlers would soon be coming to *Aotearoa* (sent there by an organization called the New Zealand Company). So the Maori agreed to sign the Treaty of Waitangi. They thought it would be good to have the protection of the British queen, as their country was attracting many lawless adventurers to its coasts – traders, sailors hunting whales and seals, and runaway convicts from the prison colonies in Australia. As long as they could live according to their customs they did not mind having some Pakeha among them, especially useful traders and missionaries who brought with them new skills in crop-growing and in reading and writing.

The signing of the Treaty of Waitangi in 1840

The Waitangi Tribunal

The Waitangi Tribunal examines Maori complaints going back to 1840, when the treaty that created New Zealand was signed. Most Maori know that the tribes cannot be paid properly for all they have lost since then. The country has not enough money. But the Maori are poorer than the Pakeha and there are ways in which their lives could be improved, and some payment made for broken promises. For instance, government support for imaginative schemes to encourage Maori education, training and the development of commercial enterprises.

was the beginning of modern New Zealand and the end of old *Aotearoa*. But the promises made to the Maoris were soon broken, as ships full of settlers arrived. By 1856 there were more Pakeha than Maori in New Zealand. The Maori tribes did not want to sell any more land to them and there was fighting between the two peoples. This fighting is now called the Land Wars. Some tribes were called rebels against the government, and their tribal lands were confiscated by the settler government.

This was a bad time for the Maori people. They had no resistance against the new diseases brought by the Pakeha. Weakened by war and disease, the Maori population was becoming smaller and smaller while the Pakeha were increasing. *'Our only duty is to smooth down their dying pillow'*, wrote the Superintendent of Wellington, one of the main settler towns. Like many others, he thought that the Maori people and their culture would soon disappear, leaving only the Pakeha way of life in New Zealand. But he was wrong. The Maori did not die. They recovered from most of the shocks of the nineteenth century. *Maoritanga* – Maori custom and belief – is still strong in New Zealand. However, the Maori are only a minority of the population now, outnumbered by the Pakeha almost ten to one.

People of the Waikato

Maui, Tuhi and Kimi are three Maori children who live with their parents, Ripeka and Hemi, in a small wooden house on the banks of the Waikato river. Hemi, their father, was once a coal miner but now he works in a big power-station beside the river. Their home is just outside a small town called Huntly, which is an unusual place. All the many other small towns in the Waikato valley are farming centres where there are markets for cows and sheep and a main street with shops selling goods for the dairy farmers of the district. Huntly is also a mining town, however, and many of the small wooden houses in the town were built for men working in the opencast coal-mines nearby.

Although Maui, Tuhi and Kimi and their parents are Maori, their way of life is similar to that of the Pakeha who live around them. Nowadays most Maori live in European-style houses and their children go to English-speaking schools along with the children of their Pakeha neighbours. They wear European-style clothes, vote in elections along with the Pakeha, watch television and play rugby and netball. But they are still proud to be Maori and in some important things their way of life remains different. They prefer some of their old customs to those brought by the Pakeha.

▲ *The modern city of Auckland lies on a narrow isthmus of land dotted with small volcanic cones. Maori tribes built fortified pa (settlements) on these cratered hills and city children can learn about New Zealand history by exploring these old pa sites.*

▲ *Maori and Pakeha children study together in New Zealand, and the younger generation of Maori are learning new skills such as computing.*

EDUCATION AND EMPLOYMENT

Hemi goes to work each day in the power-station and he enjoys his job. He tells his children that he is lucky to have it. Unemployment among the Maori people is much higher than among the Pakeha and many of the other men he knows have no work. Like many other middle-aged Maori men Hemi is an unskilled worker. When he was young few Maori boys went on from school to become apprentices and to learn skills like plumbing and electrical repair work, and even fewer went on to higher education and to university. This is one reason why unemployment is high among the Maori.

Among those people who have jobs in New Zealand the average income of Maori families is a good deal lower than that of the average Pakeha. This does not mean that the Maori feel inferior to the Pakeha, however. They know that, given the opportunity, they can do anything that the Pakeha can do. In New Zealand there

Alarming figures on Maori underdevelopment were given in 1982 in a booklet called *Race Against Time*. They showed that just over 67 per cent of Maori left school with no qualifications compared with 28.5 per cent of Pakeha New Zealanders. When the booklet was published Maori made up 9 per cent of the total population of New Zealand but 46 per cent of the prison population. Compared with the rest of the population Maori health was poor and many Maori were poorly housed. Steps have been taken to improve Maori education since then, but statistics still show the Maori to be worse off than the Pakeha in most areas of life.

▲ *Mr Koro Wetere (centre) is a Maori member of Parliament. There are four seats reserved for Maori of the ninety-five in New Zealand's Parliament: Maori can vote for these seats or for the seats that are available to anyone, Maori or Pakeha.*

are Maori politicians, doctors, writers, lawyers and engineers. Some of the politicians become Cabinet Ministers in charge of government departments. There are brilliant Maori artists – like the singer Kiri Te Kanawa – who go on to become world-famous stars. The Maori have never allowed themselves to become a servant class to the Pakeha. But the Pakeha run New Zealand according to their own values, which are often different from those of the Maori. To succeed in Pakeha society the Maori have had to turn their backs on their own customs. The best jobs, the best education and the best land in New Zealand have usually gone to the Pakeha.

Since the 1930s New Zealand has been a welfare state. There has been free health care, social welfare assistance and unemployment pay available to all the population – both Pakeha and Maori. So nobody has starved in recent times. Indeed the country became very wealthy after the Second World War, when high prices were paid by overseas buyers for its butter, cheese, meat and wool. There was enough for everybody. Times are harder now, however, because it is more difficult to sell meat and dairy produce overseas.

The Maori lost much of their land in the nineteenth century, and they also became poor compared with the Pakeha. Their complaints were largely ignored by the Pakeha until 1975, when young Maori protesters helped to organize a great Land March of Maori from all over New Zealand, down the length of the North Island. At the head of the march was Whina Cooper. Their destination was the Parliament Buildings in Wellington.

This march to draw attention to Maori land losses and other grievances was followed in 1984 by another march in the opposite direction, *Te Hikoi*. This time the Maori protesters walked from Ngaruawahia, home of the Maori King Movement, to Waitangi in the north, where the Treaty of Waitangi was signed in 1840. They called on the government to 'honour the treaty'. Once again there was a woman, or rather two women, at the head of the march – Eva Rickard and Titewhai Harawira.

THE DRIFT TO THE CITIES

There are many Maori who still live in the more remote rural parts of New Zealand, back-country areas which are often called the backblocks. Farming is more difficult now because there are no longer small dairy factories making butter and cheese in these isolated areas, and there is little profit to be made from other forms of farming. The young go to the cities where they look for work in factories, offices and wherever else jobs are available. For many of them lack of training is a handicap, and there are many problems facing the young Maori in the cities. Under the stress of town life, which is very different from the traditions of rural areas, families may break up. Tribal ties are no longer as strong as they were in the countryside. Some young Maori become homeless and some get into difficulties with the police. Crime is a big problem in the cities and can seem the only option to those with no money and lots of time.

◄ *Black, volcanic sand in a remote bay on the west coast of the North Island, where isolated farmland recently cleared from the forest is reverting to scrub again.*

▲ *Sheep farming is still important but it is harder to sell wool and mutton overseas these days. New Zealand has to find new markets and new products to survive.*

THE WORLD ECONOMY

The Maori of the remote rural areas and the Maori of the cities both face special problems. These problems have been created by change, for New Zealand as a whole is changing nowadays very rapidly. Not long ago New Zealand sold most of its goods to Britain. Some people called it Britain's 'farm in the Pacific'. Now Britain is part of the European Community, which already has too much milk, butter and meat. New Zealand has to find new products to sell to the rest of the world, and has to make new friends and trading partners, in the countries of the East as well as Europe and America.

In the Waikato valley the lives of people such as Hemi and Ripeka are affected by these changes. The Waikato depends on farming and when farming faces difficulties everyone suffers a little. Their lives have not been completely upset by change, however. The young people have not been divided from the old people. In other places such as the far north of New Zealand the young have left their tribal area to seek work far from home. But in the Waikato tribal ties have been strengthened in recent years. The Waikato Maori have had strong leaders who have encouraged new ideas in farming. They have organized co-operatives to use the strength of the tribe again, as it was used in the days when everyone worked together as one large family.

Maori population changes

In the eighteenth century when European travellers first visited *Aotearoa* there may have been 220,000 to 250,000 Maori living there. Tribal wars with European weapons and diseases introduced by the newcomers caused a terrible decline in the population. The increasing death rate was made worse by changes in lifestyle, when the Maori moved down from their healthy hill-top villages to work in swampy areas, gathering flax leaves to sell to European traders in return for guns. There was also a collapse of morale among the tribespeople as their lands were taken for Pakeha settlement and their culture and view of the world were pushed aside by the Pakeha's lifestyle.

By 1848 the Maori population may have been reduced to about 100,000. Around 1896 it reached a low point – some estimates say just under 40,000 but these figures may have been exaggerated. *'In regard to their future there is hardly a place for hope'*, wrote the English novelist Anthony Trollope. In the nineteenth century the birthrate began to climb and in the 1930s there was a dramatic improvement in Maori health. Now the Maori population is around 13 per cent of the New Zealand population of just over three million people, including many people of part-Maori part-European descent.

▲   *On the banks of the Waikato river a massed display of tribal pride as the men stamp out a haka, an action song most often used as a war dance.*

They have made plans to use hot water from Hemi's power-station to develop a fish farm run by the local Maori, but the money has not yet been found to make this plan work.

CULTURAL DIFFERENCES

Hemi has his job in the power station, but at weekends he may help on farms with other members of his tribe, if a strong arm is needed to dig crops of potatoes and *kumara* (sweet potatoes) from the ground. Sometimes he envies his unemployed friends and relatives a little, especially at the time of the year when the whitebait come up the Waikato River. Whitebait are tiny fish which swim together in large shoals. Hemi has a whitebait bench (fishing platform) among the willow trees lining a stretch of river

bank downstream. He loves to spend time there at weekends, but his unemployed friends can be on their benches during the week. Sometimes they go on expeditions at night to catch eels in streams which run into the Waikato. The Maori have always enjoyed eating smoked eels and they laugh at the Pakeha who turn up their noses at such traditional delicacies. Hemi would like to be out all night with the eel fishermen too, but he has to get back home early so he can sleep and get into work on time.

'It is not easy being a Maori in a Pakeha world', Hemi tells the children. Before the Europeans arrived the lives of the Maori were not governed by clocks. Nowadays they have modern jobs in factories, offices, farms and other workplaces, but the life of the tribe is still

▲ *The traditional Maori way is to work together, and sharing a labour project comes naturally to Maori men who are used to working with a group of relatives or friends.*

Although traditionally women were not expected by men to speak on the *marae*, in this century the Maori have often been led to campaign and to action by women. Princess Te Puea Herangi led *Kingitanga* (see pages 20-21 and 23-24), and other leaders have included Eva Rickard and Whina Cooper.

Whina Cooper (left) was at the head of the great Land March of 1975: Maori protestors from all over New Zealand marched right down North Island to the Parliament in Wellington. When she made the march, Whina Cooper was almost eighty years old.

important to most of them – even to the Maori of the city. The tribe is their family – a much bigger family than most Pakeha have. There are tribal ceremonies such as *tangihanga*, which are funeral wakes for important people who have died. Traditionally these wakes will go on for several days and distant relatives and acquaintances of the dead person are expected to gather from all over the country. If you are working in an office it is not easy to follow this tradition.

There are often clashes between the ways of the Pakeha world and tribal custom. As Hemi says, it is difficult living in both worlds at once, but like many other Maori, he has to do this.

Since the first Pakeha settlers arrived, not much more than 150 years ago, the Maori have had to change their way of life drastically. *Aotearoa* was a land of forests, but the Pakeha cut the lowland forests down. They covered much of the country with European-style farms. They even introduced birds like blackbirds, thrushes and goldfinches, and animals such as rabbits and hedgehogs, to make New Zealand seem more like a European country and less like old *Aotearoa*. The beautiful *Aotearoa* has gone, replaced by a landscape that the Pakeha created to remind them of where they came from.

▲   *Among the very young a new pride in being Maori is encouraged in kohanga reo or learning nests, where pre-school children speak nothing but Maori, and imagery from tribal legends may decorate the walls.*

Despite this, Ripeka and Hemi are bringing up their children to be proud of their *Maoritanga*. *Maoritanga* is the word used to describe Maori culture and custom – the Maori way of doing things. They are making sure that the children learn to speak Maori. Kimi goes to a *kohanga reo*, which means learning nest. This is a nursery or playgroup where the only language spoken is Maori. Many of the older people were not allowed to speak Maori at school. *Be like the Pakeha*, they were told. Some of them believed that this was best, and a few of them even tried to discourage their own children from speaking Maori.

There is a new pride in the Maori language now. More and more schools are beginning to teach Maori, to Pakeha as well as to Maori children. Some schools which once banned Maori are now using it in all their lessons, as the main language.

Ripeka and Hemi are pleased that attitudes have changed. When they were young their parents talked to them in Maori at home, but at school all their lessons were in English. Although they were intelligent children they could not keep up with their classmates who were used to speaking English all the time, and both of them were unhappy at school.

Hemi left as soon as possible, without taking any exams. He and Ripeka, who trained as a nurse and so has taken some exams, do not want this to happen to Maui, Tuhi and Kimi. *'When I was at school there was no place in the classroom for Maoritanga, the Maori way,'* Hemi recalls. *'I hope one day they will teach Maori to all Pakeha kids as well as us Maoris. How can they understand their country if they don't understand the language?'* Hemi means that almost all New Zealand's place-names are in Maori. Waikato means flowing water.

Huntly is not a Maori name but the next town up-river is called Ngaruawahia – difficult to pronounce unless you know some Maori. Ng at the beginning of a Maori word should be pronounced as the ng in sing, and each vowel pronounced separately (Ng-a-ru-a-wa-hee-a). The name comes from tribal legend and means break into food pits. Ngaruawahia is one of the most important centres of Maoridom in New Zealand; it is where the Maori queen is based.

▲ *Not so long ago the Maori language was banished from the New Zealand education system, but now things are changing and there are even meeting-houses built in school grounds, like this one at Green Bay.*

3 *Past and present*

The Waikato is New Zealand's longest river. It starts among the high volcanoes in the middle of the North Island, and flows through Lake Taupo, the biggest volcanic lake in the world. When it leaves the lake it travels through ranges of high, rugged and forested hills before flowing swiftly down into the Waikato valley.

The farmlands of the Waikato valley are often said to be the richest in the world. Tonnes of butter and cheese are made from the milk of the cows which graze on Waikato fields. The river flows through swampy country in its lower reaches and then crosses a sand-bar to enter the Tasman Sea, just south of the narrow isthmus on which Auckland, New Zealand's largest city, now stands.

Before the Pakeha arrived in New Zealand the Waikato river was a great highway for the Maori. They used the country's many rivers as their roads, travelling along them in their canoes and settling on the fertile river banks. '*Waikato of a thousand bends, at every bend a taniwha,*' was an old Maori saying. The *taniwha* is a mythical water monster, but the saying also meant that many great chiefs lived along the river. It was an important centre of Maori life

▲ *A Victorian engraving of King Tawhiao, the second Maori king. Tawhiao went into exile in the King Country after the Land Wars, but returned to the Waikato years later to make peace with the Pakeha. He is still revered as a prophet by his people.*

and the Waikato tribe was one of the most powerful tribes in *Aotearoa*.

KINGITANGA

To know why the Waikato tribe now has kings and queens, unlike any of the other tribes in New Zealand, we must look back in time to the middle of the nineteenth century. Then, many

Millions of years ago New Zealand was part of a great southern land mass. It became isolated from the rest of the world before the development of mammals. Before people arrived by sea there were no land animals there – only bats and sea mammals. It was a land of birds. Many of these birds lost the power of flight, or became clumsy fliers, because there were no predators on the ground. They include the world's only ground parrot, the kakapo, which has become very rare since humans introduced dogs, cats and rats.

In the early nineteenth century Maori tribal life was almost destroyed by two imports from Europe – the potato and the musket. The Maoris found potatoes easier to grow than their own *kumara* or sweet potatoes. They did not require so much time and attention. This meant that the men had more time to spare for tribal warfare. They bought muskets from white traders and from 1815 to 1830 the country was ravaged by the Musket Wars between the tribes.

Pakeha were arriving to settle in New Zealand. The tribes had signed the Treaty of Waitangi with the British, but they had not expected so many settlers. The treaty had promised to protect them but already much land had gone to the Pakeha, some of it unfairly, or for very little money and cheap trade goods such as axes and blankets. And still the settlers wanted more land.

In 1858 there was a meeting of many important tribes. They joined together in what they called *Kingitanga* – the Maori King Movement – and they elected a Maori king. They thought that if they united under one king, as the Pakeha were united under their queen, Victoria, they would become stronger, and better able to stop the Pakeha from taking over all of *Aotearoa*.

The warrior they chose as their king was the leading chief of the Waikato tribe, and ever since then his descendants have had the title of king or queen, and have led *Kingitanga*.

THE LAND WARS

The second half of the nineteenth century was a sad time for the Waikato Maori. There were wars between the *Kingitanga* tribes and the Pakeha over land. A British army invaded the Waikato valley and its gunboats sailed up the Waikato river. Many Pakeha and Maori were killed in battles along the river, and the Maori king and his followers retreated into the hills to the west, where they remained in exile for many years. This hilly country is still called the King Country.

▲ *To defend their territory in the 1860s the Waikato tribes built earthworked forts along the Waikato river. These were attacked by British gunboats during the Land Wars.*

No Pakeha entered the King Country but the settlers confiscated almost all the tribal land in the Waikato valley. The Waikato tribes were described as rebels by the government, and the settlers believed they deserved to lose their land. They took even the land of Maori who had not fought against the settlers in the Land Wars.

Today, the government admits that the Maori were treated unfairly. The Treaty of Waitangi should have protected their land and it did not. Over a century ago the Waikato tribespeople returned to the Waikato from exile in the King Country. The tribe received some money from the New Zealand Government for the loss of their lands, but not enough to remove the feeling of injustice. The Maori would like more land to be returned to them, and they want help to develop so that they can overcome the problems they face – problems of high unemployment, poor health, bad housing and underdevelopment. Underdevelopment means that a community has the basis to be able to provide for itself (for example land or fishing grounds) but not enough money to pay for necessary equipment (for example farm machinery or fishing nets and packing plants).

In the Waikato, Maori families such as Hemi and Ripeka and their children live happily alongside the Pakeha nowadays. The past is not often discussed, except among the Maori themselves, when they gather on their tribal *marae*. A *marae* is a meeting place. It is often just a bare patch of ground, an open space or courtyard in front of a Maori meeting-house. The language spoken on the *marae* is still Maori. At tribal meetings on the *marae* the Waikato Maori often talk about the land taken in conquest

◀ *The forested ranges of the King Country provided a haven for the Waikato Maori after their defeat in the Land Wars.*

during the nineteenth century. This includes sacred hills and rivers where the spirit of their ancestors is still strong.

Maori life today is still influenced by the events that took place 100 years ago and more. The Land Wars of the last century left tribes like the Waikatos poor and landless. Many of them felt bitter after the wars and they turned their back on Pakeha ways. This meant that in the Waikato education and healthcare suffered. For many years the people were too proud to seek Pakeha assistance in these areas, even when Maori in other parts of New Zealand were gaining university educations and some were becoming doctors, lawyers and politicians.

KINGITANGA TODAY

The person who led the Waikato Maori out of this sense of defeat and bitterness was Princess Te Puea Herangi (say Teh Poo-e-ah Hay-rah-n-gee), a member of the Waikato royal family – a grand-daughter of the first Maori King. Early this century she worked to rebuild a ceremonial capital for the Waikato Maoris and the Kingitanga tribes. She chose Ngaruawahia on the Waikato River, where the river is joined by its greatest tributary, the Waipa River. It was here that her grandfather had his *marae* and meeting-house. A Maori village is called a *pa*, and in the old days it was usually built with earthworks and wooden palisades, or fences, to

23

keep out tribal enemies. The new *pa* at Ngaruawahia was called Turangawaewae (say Too-rah-n-ga-why-why). This means a standing place or a firm foothold. Princess Te Puea wanted Ngaruawahia to be a place where the Waikato people could stand tall again.

Within the new *pa* great meeting-houses were built. The finest Maori carvers decorated them with magnificent carvings in the old tradition. Turangawaewae is now the largest *marae* and *pa* in New Zealand.

The leader of the *Kingitanga* movement and Maori queen is now Dame Te Atairangikaahu. She is called Dame because this was an honour given her by Queen Elizabeth II, Queen of Britain. She is called Dame or Queen Te Ata by many people. Her ceremonial centre is at Ngaruawahia but she lives with other members of her family in another Maori village which lies just across the Waikato River from the town of Huntly.

Throughout the Waikato there are many other *marae*, with meeting-houses which can be either grand or simple. Some are decorated with fine carvings and others are plain little wooden halls with corrugated-iron roofs and only a simple carved ancestor-figure or mask on the gable above the porch. Each large Maori tribe is made

▲   *The Maori Queen, Dame Te Atairangikaahu, speaks to a tribal gathering under carvings celebrating the coming of the Maori to Aotearoa.*

24

Traditional-style carving on the marae at Waitangi, where the Treaty creating New Zealand was signed between the British Queen and the Maori in 1840. ▶

up of several sub-tribes, and it is customary for each sub-tribe to have its own *marae* and meeting-house. It is on the *marae* that the Maori are truly in their own world again. All meeting houses and *marae* are special places where Maori people feel themselves to be in the presence of their ancestors. Indeed a meeting house is said to be shaped like a human being with head, arms and body. When you walk inside you enter the body of the tribal ancestor.

The Maori have always been great wood carvers. This art is most dramatically displayed in the large carved houses or meeting-houses, found all over New Zealand, decorated with sculptures of ancestor-figures and with creatures from tribal myth. After 1840 European travellers began arriving in New Zealand. More and more visitors demanded bigger buildings, so the modern meeting-house was created. In its design this is a combination of the old chief's houses where visitors used to be accommodated and the simple wooden churches of the first missionaries.

On the Marae

4

▲   *A naval cutter and a ceremonial war canoe landing in the Bay of Islands, where the Pakeha first settled among the Maori.*

One way in which Hemi and Ripeka and their children can keep in touch with the world of their Maori ancestors is by visiting a *marae* to take part in a *hui*, a gathering of their people.

In Maori terms, Hemi and Ripeka have a mixed marriage, for Ripeka does not come from the Waikato. She was born further north near the top of the Northland Peninsula, and belongs to the Ngapuhi tribe. She trained as a nurse when she left school, and still works part-time in Maori health schemes. Hemi met her when he

was injured at work, and had to go to hospital. In the old days the Ngapuhi and the tribes of the Waikato were fierce enemies, and there were many great tribal battles between them. Early in the nineteenth century the Ngapuhi were the first Maoris to get to know the Pakeha. Ships from Europe began visiting the Bay of Islands in Ngapuhi territory. The tribe bought muskets from the traders and with these guns they invaded other parts of *Aotearoa* including the Waikato, killing many of their old enemies.

The terrible bloodshed of those times encouraged the tribes to turn to Christianity. The missionaries offered themselves as peace-makers and the sons of some of the fiercest war leaders were converted to the new religion. Together with the missionaries they urged their people to turn their backs on warfare. Later in the nineteenth century, as the Pakeha became the largest group in New Zealand, Maori leaders called for unity among the tribes and old battles were left behind.

They are not completely forgotten. It is still not wise for a Maori to boast of past victories to a Maori from another tribe. However, Hemi gets a warm and friendly greeting nowadays when he travels north to see his Ngapuhi in-laws.

Hemi belongs to a sub-tribe of the Waikato Maori. Some kilometres to the north his sub-tribe have a little meeting house, near the Waikato River. It is a simple hall without any decorations except for a small carved ancestral mask, above the front porch. Hemi and his family and relatives gather here to mark special occasions such as weddings, twenty-first birthdays, funerals and the unveiling of memorial stones to the dead. These unveiling ceremonies are important occasions and not necessarily unhappy ones, and even at *tangihanga* or funeral wakes there is a time for laughter.

◀ *The small tribal houses on this Waikato marae demonstrate the ancient building techniques of the Maori – walls fashioned from tree-fern trunks and thickly thatched roofs.*

FEASTS

Near the meeting-house is a dining room and kitchen. When there is a *hui* or tribal gathering, the hosts always prepare a *hangi* in which they cook everyone food. A *hangi* is an earth oven – a circular hole in the ground filled with very hot stones, on which food such as pork and sweet potatoes is placed. Large quantities of food can be cooked in a *hangi*, wrapped in baskets made from leaves and covered over with leaf mats and then earth. After cooking the food comes out steaming hot and deliciously tender. The Maori have prepared feasts in this way for hundreds of years.

A favourite food at Maori feasts is *kai moana* – all kinds of seafood collected from rocky reefs and the sands along the coast, and river food such as eels, whitebait and freshwater crayfish.

The Maori know of many seafoods which are seldom tasted by the Pakeha. They know when is the best time to gather sea eggs and little octopuses and they watch the phases of the moon to select the best time to go night fishing and eeling.

TAPU AND NOA

In former times there was a very strict division in Maori life. Some things were *tapu*, or sacred and powerful, and some were *noa* – without sacred power. Cooked food was *noa*, and must never be taken into the meeting house.

A party of visitors who come to a *marae* cannot enter straight away. The *tapu* (power) they bring with them is different to that of the *marae* they are visiting. They wait outside until they hear a high-pitched wailing call coming

▲   *Steam rises from water falling on to hot rocks as helpers gingerly open a hangi or earth oven.*

▲ *Ceremonial welcomes end with a hongi or pressing of noses – a much more friendly greeting than a handshake or even a kiss on the cheek.*

from women inside. This call is a sign for them to enter. But when they go through the gates and on to the *marae* they lower their heads. The women are calling to the ancestors and the visitors hang their heads in tribute to the dead. It is always important to show respect for ancestral spirits at the start of any meeting. Then there are speeches of welcome and ceremonial chants and at the end of the welcome people shake hands and press noses.

To press noses with each other is to *hongi*. When two people *hongi* together they feel close to each other. It is a much more friendly greeting than a handshake or even a kiss on the cheek!

PUBLIC SPEAKING

Oratory – the art of speaking in public – was traditionally one of the most important arts in Maori society. Chiefs who were great orators would not stand still to speak like a Pakeha. They might dance up and down, waving in the air their carved spear or their stone club, and sometimes breaking into songs and chants.

Nowadays a good speaker on the *marae* is still fascinating to watch. Most men in the tribes did not like women to speak on the *marae* but this is changing. In recent times some of the most powerful leaders among the Maori have been women, like Princess Te Puea of the

▲   *Auckland is a multi-racial city with large Pakeha and Maori populations as well as communities from many of the Pacific islands.*

Waikatos. She had no fear of standing on the *marae* to address her people.

When Hemi goes to a gathering on his *marae* he meets many members of his wider family. Kinship is important among the Maori and even very distant relatives are considered part of the family group and are always welcome. When Hemi goes to a gathering on his *marae* he meets many distant relatives and many old friends too. Some of them now live a long way from their original home near the Waikato River. Because the Waikato tribes lost much of their land in the Land Wars there are not many Maori farmers in this area. Some of Hemi's friends and relatives have gone to the cities to find work – to Hamilton, the largest town in the Waikato valley and even

to Auckland, the biggest city in New Zealand. South Auckland has a very large Maori population, many from the Waikato.

EMPLOYMENT

Not long ago most Maori people lived in the New Zealand countryside. They began to move to the towns and cities in large numbers in the 1950s and 1960s, when they found it hard to make a living in the country. This was because farms began to use more machines and there was less work for Maori labourers. Maori people who had land found it hard to get enough money to develop their farms. In the Northland area, where Ripeka's parents still live, there are places where almost all the young people moved south to find work in Auckland during the 1960s.

In some ways the people of the Waikato were luckier. There are many large and small towns in the Waikato valley, and it was easier for Maoris seeking work to find it closer to home. Nevertheless, some of them still ended up in the big city, Auckland, in surroundings very different from those they knew in the Waikato.

Hemi's friends lucky enough to have jobs work in a wide variety of occupations. Few of them have had much education, and their work may be hard and sometimes poorly paid. He has friends and relatives who are truck drivers, and some who do seasonal farm work and who work in the market gardens which produce vegetables for Auckland. Others have jobs in the meat freezing works where sheep and cattle are killed and meat is prepared for export to Europe, the Far East and Japan. One of Hemi's cousins is a coal miner, as he was himself until he took a job as a handyman in the power-station.

Among the younger generation of Hemi's relatives, however, there are more in skilled jobs. There are several trained nurses and two teachers. Another two are office workers, and one cousin is a social worker in Auckland. One of his second cousins is training to be a newspaper reporter, which is very unusual among the Maori.

The seasonal farm workers have been finding it hard to make a good living recently, but they have not been idle. Some boast to Hemi of the amount of time they have been able to spend on their whitebait benches and what big catches they have taken.

▼ *Work takes many forms for the modern Maori, and for some it can even be a game.*

5

In the city

Hemi recently bought a car so now the family can go on expeditions at weekends to visit relatives. He is interested in tribal history and there are lots of old battle sites in or near the Waikato which he likes to explore – places like Orakau where in the Land Wars the chief Rewi Maniapoto was surrounded by the British Army. Rewi had about 320 supporters in his *pa* when 1,800 Pakeha soldiers arrived to try to capture it. Three times the Pakeha attacked the *pa* and three times they were beaten back. When the Maori had hardly any ammunition left the British commander called on them to surrender.

'*We will fight on*', the Maoris cried, '*for ever, for ever, for ever!*'

One Sunday Hemi and Ripeka loaded the children and a picnic lunch into the car and drove south to Orakau, which lies on the edge of the King Country. They found the monument which stands by the roadside, showing where the Battle of Orakau took place. Hemi told the children that his great-great-grandmother had been in Rewi's stockade at Orakau, and had fought the soldiers along with the other women in the *pa*. After the men had refused to surrender, the British commander called on them to let the women leave the *pa*. Then the women shouted that they would fight on forever too.

'*You can be proud of your tupuna*', Hemi tells the children. *Tupuna* means ancestors. The ancestors have always been important to the Maori and some people can still recite a list of all their *tupuna* going back to the canoe which first brought them to *Aotearoa*.

Hemi's great-great-grandmother escaped from Orakau along with Rewi Maniapoto and other Maori survivors of the battle, and their story became famous all over New Zealand – among the Pakeha as well as the Maori.

Beside the roadside, Hemi says a prayer in

◀ *The Maori were expert designers of earthworked fortifications and all over New Zealand there are terraced hills which were once tribal strongholds. During the Land Wars many Pakeha soldiers died trying to storm them.*

Maori soldiers suffered heavy casualties during the Second World War, when a volunteer unit went overseas. The Maori Battalion was famous for its courage and for its fierce bayonet charges.

In North Africa a young Maori lieutenant, Moana-nui-a-kiwa Ngarimu, became the first of his people to win Britain's highest medal, the Victoria Cross, awarded after his death. He died in a hand-to-hand battle defending a rocky hill. In another part of North Africa the Maori Battalion stormed a cliff to capture a German stronghold, as their ancestors had stormed hill forts in the days of tribal battles. At home in New Zealand the Maori Battalion song became for a while the most popular tune of the war.

Maori for his great-great-grandmother and her comrades. Then they leave Orakau to find a place to picnic beside the Puniu River, the old King Country frontier.

Some weekends the family drive to the seaside. On the Tasman coastline there are harbours like Kawhia, where there are sheltered waters and safe places to swim. At Kawhia they can visit a place sacred to the Waikato Maori. This is a mound near the shore, under which the Tainui canoe is buried. The Waikato Maori belong to a group of tribes who all call themselves

▲ *This protester calling on the government to honour the Treaty of Waitangi uses a war memorial as his backdrop.*

◀ *Nobody can be sure exactly how the Maori first came to Aotearoa, but many artists have painted pictures of a fleet of canoes setting sail from islands in the Pacific. The canoe that brought the Tainui tribes to Aotearoa is supposed to have land at Kawhia.*

the Tainui people. All these tribes believe that their first ancestors came to *Aotearoa* in the Tainui canoe.

The canoe arrived in Kawhia Harbour and then the Tainui people spread from the coast over the hills into the Waikato valley. They also travelled from the Waikato to the Pacific coast and settled along the Hauraki Gulf.

One place Hemi has rarely visited is Auckland, although the city is only an hour's drive away from Huntly and Hemi's cousin Tupu lives there. Auckland is the largest city in New Zealand. Many of the Maori who have left their tribal lands to work in the city now live in Auckland, especially in the suburb called Otara.

As well as Maori people, there are many people living in Otara who have come to work in New Zealand from the Pacific islands. Most of these islands are Polynesian, and the people speak languages which are related to Maori. In Otara there is a famous market where you can buy fruit and vegetables from all over the Pacific.

In 1982 New Zealand's Race Relations Conciliator published statistics which showed that 46 per cent of the prison population was Maori and nearly 50 per cent of all the criminal cases involved Maori. At that time only about 9 per cent of the New Zealand population was Maori. More recent statistics still show the proportion of Maori in jail to be over seven times the national average. Crime among the Maori rose sharply in the 1960s and 1970s as people moved to the cities. Crime in many societies is highest among the young and the lower wage earning groups and the Maori population in the cities was very young and often poor.

The Race Relations Conciliator said in 1982 that the New Zealand police had come under severe criticism from Maori and Pacific Polynesian communities. These communities felt they were being unequally singled out by harsh police methods. In street inquiries the police seemed to pick on Maori and Pacific Polynesians, who were more likely to end up before the courts for minor offences than the Pakeha.

TUPU

Sometimes Tupu, Hemi's cousin, comes to stay with Hemi and Ripeka at Huntly. When he was young he lived for some years in Hemi's house and the two are like brothers. It is common in Maori families for children to live with uncles, aunts and grandparents rather than staying always with their own parents. Tupu brings with him presents from Auckland. Once he brought some beautiful cloth printed with Pacific designs

◀ *In Otara market you can buy sweet potatoes, yams and fruit from all over the Pacific.*

which he found in Otara market.

Tupu first went to live in Auckland when he was a teenager. His family did not want him to go. '*I was pretty wild then*', he tells Maui and Tuhi when they ask him about his life in Auckland. '*Everybody seemed to be going to the city. I wanted to see what it was like*'. He went to stay with relatives who lived in Ponsonby, near the centre of the city. But he quarrelled with his relatives, and left their house. Like a lot of young Maori he felt lost in the city.

He missed the warmth of life in the country. In the country there were lots of friends and relatives around, and there were also the elders of his tribe, who always keep an eye on young people like Tupu. The elders would quickly tell him if they thought he was doing the wrong thing. In the city there was no one to give him advice. Like a lot of young Maori in the city he wanted the close companionship of tribal life but wasn't sure how to get it. He joined a Maori gang, because he felt safer and more at ease in a group.

The gang system began to develop in New Zealand after thousands of young Maori moved to the towns and cities in the 1960s and 1970s. Many of these young people lost touch with their tribal roots. They had no elders in the cities and they felt ill at ease and even angry in a world where the Pakeha seemed to have all the money and power. The young Maori often had difficulty getting jobs. The gangs they formed were like the motor-cycle gangs of America – the Hell's Angels. They called themselves the Stormtroopers, the Nigs and Junior Nigs, the Spades, Black Power, the Tribe, the Mongrels and the Panthers. Sometimes they lived together in houses which they fortified so they seemed to be like the old fighting *pa*.

The gangs frightened the Pakeha and they frightened and worried many of the older Maori in the countryside. They were not all bad and dangerous, however. There were young men in

▲ *When Maori gangs developed in New Zealand's cities in the 1970s Nazi insignia were popular. One group called themselves the Stormtroopers.*

some of the gangs like Tupu, who could see that the Maori people were poorer than the Pakeha, and that Maori health was often poor too. Maori went to prison more than Pakeha. These things made them angry, but what could they do?

TE HIKOI

In 1983 Tupu met one of his relatives in Auckland, who had come from Waahi *pa*, across the Waikato River from Huntly. Waahi is the village where the Maori Queen has her home. Tupu's relative told him that at Waahi they were planning a great march of Maoris from all over New Zealand. They wanted to tell the Pakeha about the problems facing the Maori, and to draw attention to the Treaty of Waitangi, which had made so many promises to the Maori tribes that had not been kept.

The Maori wanted the Government to honour the treaty. They thought that if they all marched to Waitangi, where the treaty was signed in 1840, the Pakehas might listen to their grievances. They wanted the Government to plan for Maori development, and they wanted the return of more Maori land.

Tupu and some of his gang decided to go on the march, which the Maoris called *Te Hikoi*. With hundreds of others they walked for a fortnight, from Ngaruawahia to Waitangi. They slept in meeting houses and heard speeches on the *marae*. Tupu talked with famous Maori leaders on the march. Some of them told him he should make better use of his intelligence and energy than he had been doing. Tupu thought

Maori MPs

The Pakeha settlers in New Zealand were allowed their first parliament in 1852 by the British Government. In 1867 it was decided that four Maori members should be elected by the Maori people to represent the northern, western, eastern and southern Maori. Nowadays there are still four Maori members of the ninety-five member parliament. Maori voters can choose to switch from the Maori to the general electoral roll if they wish, to vote for the same candidates as their Pakeha neighbours.

▼ *In 1984 Maori from all over New Zealand took part in Te Hikoi, a protest march to the Treaty Grounds at Waitangi. They carried with them the banners of Te Kotahitanga – the Maori unity movement.*

▲ *Police block the road to Waitangi as Maori protesters head for the Treaty Grounds in 1984.*

about this for some time, and then decided to enter a training scheme when the *Hikoi* was over.

Now he is a social worker. He still knows many gang members. Sometimes he helps them when they are in trouble, but most of his work is done among the street kids of Auckland. Street kids are young homeless people, mostly from Maori or from Pacific islander families. They are to be found in New Zealand's cities, sometimes sleeping in rough shelters. The street kids have often run away from troubles at home. There may have been little room for them in crowded housing with unemployed brothers, sisters and cousins. Some Maori in the cities feel that they are surrounded by a culture that is different from their own. They cannot get a job or a decent place to live, and this makes them feel that they are worthless. Some of them get drunk to try to get rid of this feeling of worthlessness. Many street kids have run away from homes where their parents or relatives drank too much. The street kids who run away for these reasons are even more lost than Tupu was when he first found himself alone in Auckland.

At home in the Waikato Maui and Tuhi listen to Tupu's stories about the street kids. Perhaps Auckland is not such a wonderful place after all, they think. They ask him about *Te Hikoi*. What happened when all the Maori marchers got to Waitangi?

'It was a great disappointment', says Tupu. The Pakeha were celebrating Waitangi Day when they arrived, but the marchers were kept away from the Waitangi celebrations. They were not allowed to speak to the governor general and the prime minister. They had hoped to do that, but they had also promised that *Te Hikoi* would be a peace march. Nobody made trouble at Waitangi. Even the gang members kept the promise to be peaceful, though they danced *haka* (war dances) in a field and made fiery speeches.

The protestors went home from Waitangi thinking the *Hikoi* had been a failure. A few months later, however, the National Party lost the elections to the Labour Party, and a new government came to power which promised to examine the grievances which the Maori marchers had taken to Waitangi.

'Once none of us Maori talked to the Pakehas about the lands that we lost', Hemi tells the children. *'We always thought nobody was listening. But now people are beginning to listen to us. We Maori can change things if we have the courage of our ancestors.'*

Maori tribal groups and individuals have successfully challenged the government in the courts and the Waitangi Tribunal in recent years, forcing changes of policy on a number of issues. In 1983 Aila Taylor, a butcher from the Taranaki town of Waitara, won a case he brought before the Waitangi Tribunal.

He claimed that a large scale industrial development sponsored by the government would destroy his tribe's fishing reefs. It therefore broke the promises of the Treaty of Waitangi. The government agreed to try to protect the reefs. Since then tribal groups have won other major cases brought before the Tribunal, about rights to land and to fisheries. In many of these cases there is still no final agreement on what steps should be taken to right the wrongs of the past.

▼ *The site of Raglan golf course, overlooking Raglan Harbour, was won back for the Maori after a long struggle by Eva Rickard.*

The four winds

6

The Maori sometimes call themselves *Nga Hau e Wha*, the tribes of the four winds, because they can be divided into the northern, eastern, western and southern peoples.

THE WEST WIND

The Waikato Maori belong to the western group and live in a part of New Zealand which is the most prosperous and heavily populated in the country. The rolling farmlands of the Waikato are very different in appearance to some other parts of New Zealand.

The sea coasts have always been important to the Maori. There used to be a heavy population of tribes in the Taranaki province of the North Island. Taranaki has fertile farmlands pushing out in a bulge into the Tasman Sea around the base of spectacular volcano, called by the Maori Taranaki and by the Pakeha Mount Egmont. Here, as in the Waikato, much tribal land was confiscated from the tribes after the Land Wars. But the local Maori still use the rich reefs along the coastline as a source of food, particularly for feeding visitors who come to the great Manukorihi *pa* at Waitara. They have fought a brave campaign to stop these reefs being polluted by heavy industry. Taranaki Maori are part of the west wind tribal grouping, like the Waikatos.

THE EAST WIND

In the centre of the North Island is a high volcanic plateau. From the plateau rise three giant volcanoes, Ruapehu, Tongariro and Ngauruhoe. Smoke and steam still hiss from vents in their snow-clad summits, and sometimes the snow is blackened by volcanic cinders and ash. Around the plateau are broken ranges of rugged hills, some still heavily forested. The mountainous ranges east of the volcanic region are still home to people like the Tuhoe. Long

◀ *The peaks rising above Milford Sound are the most spectacular in Fiordland, part of South Island.*

after many other tribes had adapted themselves to the ways of the Pakeha, Maori language and custom remained strong among the Tuhoe. Around the East Cape are other tribes. Some of these tribes of the east wind held on to much of their land, unlike the Waikato people. This century they have become farmers in the Pakeha way, rearing sheep and cattle.

THE NORTH WIND

The Northland Peninsula which pushes northwards into the Pacific from the Auckland isthmus is the home of the northern peoples. They include two large tribes, the Ngati Whatua and the Ngapuhi. Their region of New Zealand

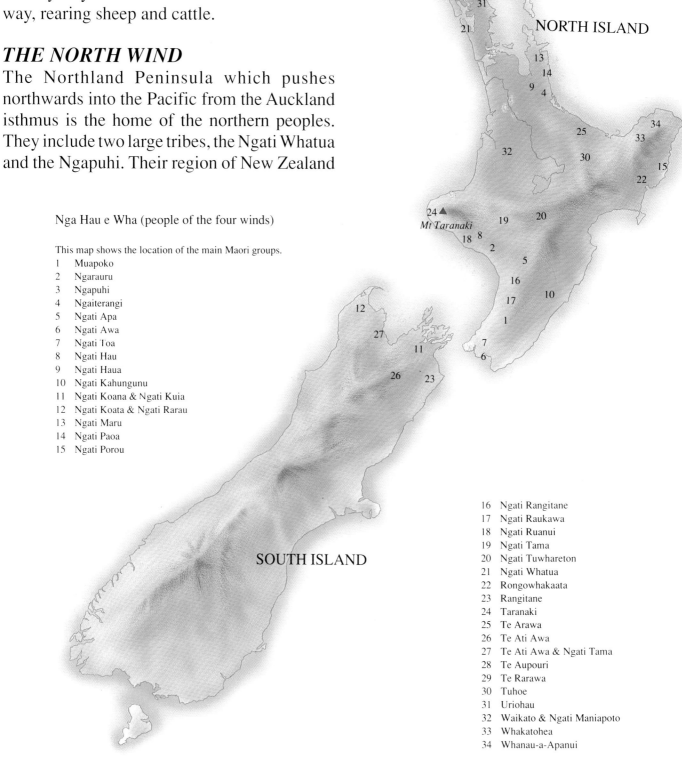

Nga Hau e Wha (people of the four winds)

This map shows the location of the main Maori groups.
1   Muapoko
2   Ngarauru
3   Ngapuhi
4   Ngaiterangi
5   Ngati Apa
6   Ngati Awa
7   Ngati Toa
8   Ngati Hau
9   Ngati Haua
10 Ngati Kahungunu
11 Ngati Koana & Ngati Kuia
12 Ngati Koata & Ngati Rarau
13 Ngati Maru
14 Ngati Paoa
15 Ngati Porou

16 Ngati Rangitane
17 Ngati Raukawa
18 Ngati Ruanui
19 Ngati Tama
20 Ngati Tuwhareton
21 Ngati Whatua
22 Rongowhakaata
23 Rangitane
24 Taranaki
25 Te Arawa
26 Te Ati Awa
27 Te Ati Awa & Ngati Tama
28 Te Aupouri
29 Te Rarawa
30 Tuhoe
31 Uriohau
32 Waikato & Ngati Maniapoto
33 Whakatohea
34 Whanau-a-Apanui

▲ *Taranaki, a dormant volcano, is the sacred mountain of the Taranaki Maori. It is called Mount Egmont by the Pakeha.*

is sometimes called the winterless north because it is so warm. You seldom get even a frost in Northland, and it was the area where the early Maori found it easiest to grow the plants they brought from the warm Pacific islands – the *kumara* or sweet potato, the yam and the taro – a tropical plant with an edible root.

THE SOUTH WIND

The need for warmth in which to grow their plants meant that many Maori lived in the north, and along the sunny and fertile eastern coasts of the North Island. Far fewer tribes are to be found in the South Island, a much colder region. The most widespread southern tribe is the Ngai Tahu. During the Musket Wars many of the

South Island Maori were killed by northern Maori, so many Maori in the South Island are branches of the West Wind tribes who moved there after the Musket Wars.

In the South Island there are high snow-capped mountains, wide tussock-covered plains and an area round the southern coast which is called Fiordland. Fiordland is still an empty country of wild forest-covered mountains rising steeply from deep inlets of the sea.

Ripeka was born in Northland, a member of the Ngapuhi tribe. That means she belongs to the north wind grouping. She and Hemi and the children recently went to her tribe's home in the Northland for a family wedding. Hemi drove everyone to Auckland, where they all stayed with Tupu in Otara before travelling on to Ripeka's family village, near the Bay of Islands.

Tupu guided them through Auckland and over the harbour bridge to the road leading north. With stops for lunch and a swim on the Pacific coast it took them over six hours to reach Ripeka's home village. The children found the northern landscape strange and fascinating. Just north of Auckland the road runs along a high ridge of hills. Down below are inlets of the sea with acres of mud-flats alongside the tidal creeks. Thousands of mangrove trees dot the mud-flats, half submerged in salt water when the tide comes in. They passed patches of forest in which they saw giant kauri trees. There are hills covered in tall tree-ferns and nikau palms. It looks much more tropical than the Waikato.

THE BAY OF ISLANDS

Ripeka's parents live just south of the Bay of Islands in a valley near the sea. Several car-loads of Hemi's relatives travelled north to attend the wedding, and in the evening there was a ceremonial welcome – a *mihi* – for the guests from the Waikato, on the *marae*. The visitors replied with speeches and chants and a song in Maori which everyone including the children joined in. That night they slept in a little meeting-house, lying on foam mattresses arranged in rows along the walls.

Many of their Ngapuhi hosts stayed in the meeting-house too, and they all talked until late at night, sometimes dropping off to sleep and then waking to join in the conversation again. Early next morning Maui, Tuhi and Kimi went

▲ *A haka being performed as part of a welcoming ceremony.*

42

exploring before some of the old people were awake. There is a big hill behind the meeting house dotted with huge smooth rocks. The children knew they had to keep to the path and not climb these rocks as they have always been *tapu*. They may hide caves containing old burial sites or even be objects thought to contain the soul of a dead person.

The children kept well clear of them. They followed a small stream down into a valley and then climbed another hill. At the top were strange earthworked ditches. It is an old *pa* site. This was the fortified hill-top village where Ripeka's ancestors lived, overlooking a coastal bay and the blue Pacific.

There are many Maori people like Ripeka's parents in New Zealand, still living close to

▲   *This is a re-creation of the old-style chief's hut where visitors to the pa were accommodated before the modern meeting-house was developed.*

In a Maori tribe in the old days work was communal. Everyone joined in activities such as planting and looking after the growing crops. When Pakeha came they changed *Aotearoa* into a country of small farms raising sheep and cattle, each one owned by only one person or one family. Recently some tribal groups in the Waikato and on the east coast have tried a return to communal farming. They have moved away from the one-person farm to organize collectives, claiming back Maori land leased to Pakeha farmers and pooling the labour and skills of tribal members.

▲ *Shellfish called pipi are plentiful in the sands of many sheltered bays.*

▼ *Hangi – earth ovens that are big enough to cook a whole pig inside – are prepared by the Maori for special feasts with many people present.*

where their ancestors dwelt. For them the tribal landscape is still full of ancestor spirits and each hill and rock may have a special meaning.

The wedding took place in a small wooden church, and was followed by a feast at Ripeka's family *pa*. The Waikato group had arrived a day before the celebration. The children had watched people prepare the *hangi*, and helped fetch firewood. A big fire was lit to heat stones for the oven. Later their grandmother had taken them to the nearby beach. They dug in the sand for little shellfish called *pipi*, while their relatives stood in waist-high water groping for seafood on rocky reefs. These delicacies were all eaten the next day.

In Ripeka's Northland valley the population has declined. It is only for celebrations such as the wedding that many of the younger men and women return. Much of the land in this part of the north is owned by Maori farmers. The local dairy factory has closed, however, and some of

◀ *Kiwi fruit – one of the crops developed by New Zealand farmers in their search for new overseas markets.*

the farmlands in the valley are abandoned to scrub again. The younger farmers have gone to the city.

THE FUTURE

In the old days the Maori depended on food from the forests – berries and birds – as well as their cultivated plants and on fish and shellfish. When tribal land went to the Pakeha and the forests were cut down they had to change their way of life to survive.

Happily the Maori people have a special quality which they showed when they learned how to farm with new plants and animals from Europe. They can quickly adapt – they have never been frightened of change. Their ancestors moved across the Pacific from one island to the next, never knowing what was lying over the horizon. The modern Maori have moved on bravely too, and they are building new *marae* and meeting-houses in the cities now. This suggests that they are there to stay, but some will probably eventually return to the country, to quiet spots like Ripeka's valley. Such places can flower again. The old-time Maori were expert at coaxing difficult tropical plants to grow in *Aotearoa*'s cool climate. New Zealand needs such skills now. Kiwi fruit are taking over from cows on some farms and more and more strange plants are being grown for export. For explorers like the Maori there is always a new horizon, a new challenge.

Glossary of Maori words

Aotearoa   Land of the Long White Cloud, a Maori name for New Zealand.
Hangi   An earth oven filled with hot stones.
Hawaiki   The mythical homeland from which the ancestors of the Maori came to *Aotearoa*.
Hongi   To greet someone by pressing noses with them.
Hui   A gathering of people, meeting.
Kai moana   Freshwater and seafood traditionally eaten by the Maori.
Kingitanga   The Maori King Movement.
Kohanga reo   A language nest, a Maori language play-group for pre-school children.
Kumara   Sweet potato.
Maoritanga   Maori custom and culture, the Maori way of doing things.
Marae   An open space, a courtyard for the conduct of ceremonies, usually in front of a meeting-house. Also the settlement around the courtyard.
Mihi   A ceremonial welcome.
Noa   Powerless, not sacred.
Pa   A fortified Maori stronghold or village.
Pakeha   A European or white person, or any non-Maori.
Tangihanga   A traditional Maori wake for someone who has died.
Taniwha   A mythical water monster.
Tapu   Sacred, forbidden, sacred power.
Tupuna   Ancestors.

Glossary of English words

Apprentice   Someone who works for another person or company in order to learn a trade, such as carpentry.
Colonist   See settler.
Colony   Territory that a powerful country has claimed as its own, sending government officials there and taking control of the administration of the area.
Earthworked   Built of earth.
Flax   A sword-leaved plant that commonly grows in New Zealand. The fibres of the stems are woven into linen cloth.
Haven   Safe place.
Isthmus   A narrow strip of land between two larger areas.
Kinship   Family relationship. People can be part of a family through descent, marriage and adoption. In Western society kinship groups are usually quite small and based on descent. Among many non-Western societies, among them the Maori, kinship groups are much larger.
Land Wars   The wars between Maori tribes and Pakeha in the nineteenth century.
Mixed marriage   A marriage between people who come from different races or nations or peoples.
Polynesia   A region of the Pacific Ocean, including New Zealand, Hawaii and the Samoan islands.
Settler   Someone who moves to a different place to live there. In this book, settlers are the Pakeha who came to live in New Zealand in the nineteenth century.
Tribunal   A place where judgements are made about which side is right in a dispute.
Underdevelopment   Lack of money with which to develop resources.
Wake   A gathering soon after someone has died, when the dead person's relatives meet to remember him or her.

Further reading

For older readers:

A History of New Zealand, Keith Sinclair (Allen Lane & Pelican Books, London, 1980)
(Although now quite old and difficult to get hold of this is an excellent general history.)

The Maori of Aotearoa – New Zealand, A Minority Rights Group Report, (Minority Rights Group, London, 1990)

Te Marae: A Guide to Custom and Protocol, Hiwi & Pat Tauroa
(Reed Books, Auckland 1991)

Nga Tau Tohetohe - Years of Anger, Ranginui Walker (Penguin Books (NZ) Ltd., 1987)

Whina – A Biography of Whina Cooper, Michael King (Hodder & Stoughton, 1983)

For younger readers:

Maori Myths and Legends: Land of the Long White Cloud, Kiri Te Kanawa (Pavilion Books, 1989)

Maoris, Hilary Lee-Corbin (Wayland, 1989) A more junior introduction to the Maori.

New Zealand, Andrew Kelly (Wayland, 1989)

Further information

In New Zealand:

Maori Education Foundation, PO Box 3745 Wellington, New Zealand.

Waitangi Tribunal, Department of Justice (Waitangi Tribunal Division), PO Box 5022, Wellington, New Zealand.

Centre for Maori Studies, Waikato University, Private Bag, Hamilton, New Zealand.

In Britain:

The Minority Rights Group has an education project that produces learning material and information for teachers covering many aspects of minority rights. For more information contact:

Minority Rights Group
379 Brixton Rd
London SW9 7DE

Index

Numbers in **bold** refer to pictures as well as text.